REBOOT

REBOOT

IF THAT DOESN'T WORK, PLUG IT IN!

JOSHUA CALHOUN

TATE PUBLISHING
AND ENTERPRISES, LLC

Reboot
Copyright © 2013 by Joshua Calhoun. All rights reserved.

No part of this publication may be reproduced, stored in a retrieval system or transmitted in any way by any means, electronic, mechanical, photocopy, recording or otherwise without the prior permission of the author except as provided by USA copyright law.

This novel is a work of fiction. However, several names, descriptions, entities, and incidents included in the story are based on the lives of real people.

The opinions expressed by the author are not necessarily those of Tate Publishing, LLC.

Published by Tate Publishing & Enterprises, LLC
127 E. Trade Center Terrace | Mustang, Oklahoma 73064 USA
1.888.361.9473 | www.tatepublishing.com

Tate Publishing is committed to excellence in the publishing industry. The company reflects the philosophy established by the founders, based on Psalm 68:11,
"The Lord gave the word and great was the company of those who published it."

Book design copyright © 2013 by Tate Publishing, LLC. All rights reserved.
Cover design by Allen Jomoc
Interior design by Mary Jean Archival

Published in the United States of America

ISBN: 978-1-62746-600-4
1. Humor / Topic / Business & Professional
2. Computers / Reference
13.07.22

CONTENTS

Preface 7
The Super Router... 9
The Hacker and His Vacuum 10
Get a Better Seat 11
No Signal... 12
The Dark Side... 13
Merry Christmas 14
Kryptonite 15
Luxury Computers.. 16
The Infamous How-To 17
MFDs—Multiple Failing Devices 18
Confusing Buttons.. 19
I Can't Live Without My Phone!....................................... 20
Registering Your Warranty 21
It's All a Matter of Per-Spectrum 22
When Doesn't It Work?... 23
DVD Fail... 24
Proof That 12/21/12 Is Not the End!................................ 25
No, It's the Women's Urinal.. 26
Yummy 27
She's a Real Knockout! 28
It's the Simple Things 29
Yes, We Get Prank Calls.. 30
Flip Flop.. 31

Lying Doesn't Pay	32
Freezing Hot	33
Chocolate and Grief Counseling	34
Knowing Your Ins and Outs	35
Under Communicator-n-ing	36
Hue Need Glasses	37
Anyone Have a CVD?	38
The Power of the Power Button	39
Comma, On!	40
The Indefinite Loop	41
Rechanging	42
Disappearing Act	43
Selective Hearing	44
Shut Down a.k.a. Off	45
Step 3: See Step 1	46
Breaking Glass	47
The Precall Call	48
Magneto Makes a House Call	49
Conclusion	51
Troubleshooting Guide	53
Troubleshooting Power Issues	54
Troubleshooting Network Issues	62
Troubleshooting CD/DVD Issues	65
Troubleshooting Printer Issues	68
Troubleshooting Microsoft Office	69
Troubleshooting Virus/Malware	70

PREFACE

All stories are true, but they have been slightly altered to protect the identity of organizations for security purposes. All numbers have been altered, and names have been left out.

This is a compilation of actual calls, tickets, and events that tech support agents receive. Some of these stories are humorous; however, others are serious or just plain interesting.

The point of this book is not to poke fun at the callers but to help many realize that they are not the only ones out there who have had issues like this. Many of these same calls are received on a daily basis. Some people just get nervous on the phone. That's okay. You're not alone.

Enjoy the stories. I hope they help answer questions or resolve issues you may be having.

As a bonus, provided at the end of the book is a troubleshooting guide that will help with the majority of your technical issues. The exact steps that tech support would walk you through are listed. Hopefully, they will save you a phone call.

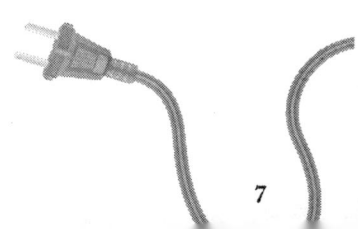

THE SUPER ROUTER

Agent: Thanks for calling tech support. How may I help you?
Caller: Yes, my laptop won't turn on.
Agent: What does it do when you push the Power button?
Caller: The light just flashes a few times, and then nothing happens.
Agent: Is the laptop plugged in?
Caller: Yes, we just had the router hooked up and everything!
Agent: No, the power cord, is it plugged in?
Caller: Yes, the router is hooked up and everything!
Agent: The black box that goes from the wall to the computer, is that plugged in?

Caller plugs in the power cord, and the laptop turns on.

Caller: So do you mean to tell me that the router does not charge my computer?
Agent: No, ma'am, the wireless router does not charge your computer.

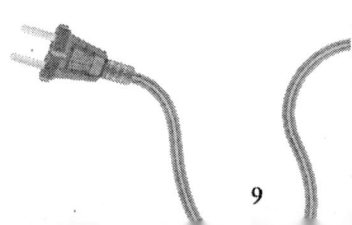

THE HACKER AND HIS VACUUM

Agent: Thanks for calling tech support. How may I help you?
Caller: Someone is hacking into my computer, and they have been following me since my last address.
Agent: How do you know the—
Caller: (Interrupts agent) Because the apartment above me has scanners! They hack into my cell phone. People are coming into my house when I'm not around and leave candy wrappers everywhere. They did the same thing at my last house! They've been following me. They get on my computer, and I have to beep into my computer to change my password every thirty days. I have had severe injuries because of the booby traps they leave in my apartment. They have also hacked into my electricity and cable. When I came back the other day, I found my TV off! I'm collecting their code so I can take it to the police station. They are working in shifts. I know the maintenance guy is in on it because he keeps coming by the room vacuuming!
Agent: Ah...
Caller: Here they come!
Click.

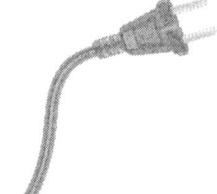

GET A BETTER SEAT

Agent: Thanks for calling tech support. How may I help you?
Caller: I can't get a signal, but my friend can.
Agent: Is your friend next to you?
Caller: Yes.
Agent: Are they using an air card or connecting to a router?
Caller: Well, I don't know. I mean, they're three hundred yards away from me."

Note: Three hundred yards is the size of three football fields. Most home routers can't send a signal over half a football field away.

Agent: Um... That would probably be why you can't get a signal.
Caller: Oh, so that's too far?
Agent: Yeah, that's... that's too far.

NO SIGNAL

Agent: Thanks for calling tech support. How may I help you?
Caller: I can't get online.
Agent: What happens when you open Internet Explorer?
Caller: It says "No Signal."
Agent: Okay, click on Start.
Caller: I can't because I'm not online.
Agent: Do you see a Windows icon in the bottom left corner?
Caller: No, it just says "No Signal."
Agent: Is the computer on?
Caller: Yes, but it just says "No Signal."

Note: Most monitors will say "No Signal" when the monitor is on, but the computer is not.

Agent: Are there any lights on the computer? The black box with the CD drive, that is probably on the ground or under the desk.
Caller: No.
Agent: Okay, look for the Power button on that box and push it.

Caller pushes the button, and the computer turns on.

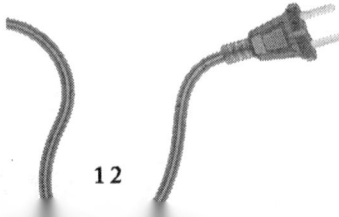

THE DARK SIDE

Agent: Thanks for calling tech support. How may I help you?
Caller: My mouse won't move on my laptop.
Agent: Have you tried restarting the laptop?
Caller: Yes, whenever I start it, the mouse is black.
Agent: What do you see on the screen?
Caller: A black mouse.
Agent: Other than the mouse, what do you see?
Caller: Nothing, it won't let me go anywhere because the mouse is black.
Agent: Is the computer on?
Caller: I think so. I pushed the Power button.
Agent: Where's the AC Adapter? Is it plugged in?
Caller: No, I had to unplug it when I spilled my drink.
Agent: Did that drink get on the computer?
Caller: No, just the keyboard.
Agent: Okay, the motherboard is probably damaged too because it's under the keyboard.
Caller: But wouldn't the mouse still work?
Agent (after a long pause): Probably not. Let's set that up for repair.

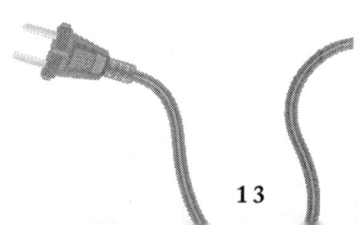

MERRY CHRISTMAS

Agent: Thanks for calling tech support. How may I help you?
Caller: Yes, please help me. I just got my computer back from repair. It was gone for three weeks, and I just got it back, and it won't turn on.
Agent: Okay, is it a desktop or a laptop?
Caller: Desktop.
Agent: Unplug the power cord from the wall and the computer, and plug it back in.

Caller plugged it in, and it turned on.

Caller: Oh, thank you so much. You don't know how much this means. My son has been in Afghanistan for the past two years. I haven't been able to talk to him for the past three weeks because my computer was at the shop. It's Christmas weekend, and if you hadn't helped me get the computer to turn on, I wouldn't have been able to talk to my son on Christmas. Thank you so much.
Agent (almost in tears): You're so welcome. Have fun talking with your son, and Merry Christmas.

KRYPTONITE

Agent: Thanks for calling tech support. How may I help you?
Caller: Hi, my computer doesn't work right.
Agent: What is it doing?
Caller: It just never works right unless I'm next to the crystals. It only works when it's next to the crystals, so I want to send it in for repair.
Agent: What is it doing right now?
Caller: Well, it's working fine right now, but that's just because I'm next to the crystals.
Agent: What does it do when it's not by the crystals?
Caller: Well, if I take it away from the crystals, it won't work!
Agent: Can you give me an example of what it does or does not do when it is not next to the crystals?
Caller: No! I can't!
Click.

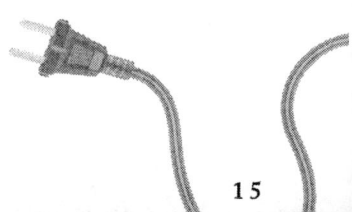

LUXURY COMPUTERS

Agent: Thanks for calling tech support. How may I help you?
Caller: Hi, yes, I'm calling in because my cup holder stopped working.
Agent: You're cup holder?
Caller: Yes, you know the little tray that pops in and out of the computer. It won't go back in anymore.
Agent: Sir, that's a CD player.
Caller: I'm trying to think of a CD. Is that the round one?
Agent: Yes, with the hole in the center.
Caller: Oh.

THE INFAMOUS HOW-TO

Agent: Thanks for calling tech support. How may I help you?
Caller: Yes, I need help transferring a homemade movie from a DVD to my computer.
Agent: I apologize, sir, but that is not something that is covered by the manufacturer's warranty.
Caller: I hope you people rot in hell!
Click.

Agent turns to colleague.

Agent: This guy just said, "I hope you people rot in hell" because I couldn't help him transfer his homemade DVD to his computer.
Colleague: Did you tell him the way to salvation was through Google?

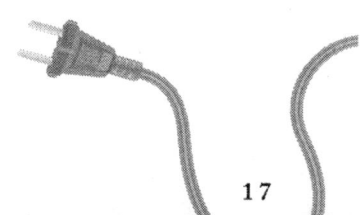

MFDS—MULTIPLE FAILING DEVICES

Agent: Thanks for calling tech support. How may I help you?
Caller: I'm having trouble sending a fax.
Agent: Okay, let's send a test fax.
Caller: Ok, I sent you a copy...Wait, now it's printing out my receipt... It's printing another receipt, and now it says 3/63! Whatever the heck that means.
Agent: Ah, sir, press the red Cancel button. It was making sixty-three copies. You need to send a fax.

CONFUSING BUTTONS

Agent: Thanks for calling tech support. How may I help you?
Caller: Hi. I'm having trouble with my printer, and I can't figure out what these buttons do.
Agent: What do the buttons say?
Caller: They say Print, Copy, and Scan.
Agent: …

I CAN'T LIVE WITHOUT MY PHONE!

Agent: Thanks for calling tech support. How may I help you?
Caller: Hi, my phone won't turn on.
Agent: Have you tried turning it on while it's plugged into the charger?
Caller: Yes. It won't turn on there either.
Agent: Okay, we will be sending you a check to replace your phone. It should arrive within five to seven business days.
Caller: So you mean to tell me I will be without a phone for a week?
Agent: I apologize, sir, but you will get the full amount for the phone back.
Caller: I can't live without my phone! Can you send it any quicker?
Agent: I apologize, sir, but that's the only option I have with this type of warranty.
Caller: Fine, give me the confirmation number.
Agent: Okay, your confirmation number is...
Caller: Hang on. Hang on. I'm trying to type this into my other iPhone.

REGISTERING YOUR WARRANTY

Agent: Thanks for calling tech support. How may I help you?
Caller: Yes, I need to register my warranty.
Agent: Okay, do you have the purchase date?
Caller: I don't see the purchase date on here. It does show the day that I bought it though.
Agent: ...

IT'S ALL A MATTER OF PER-SPECTRUM

Agent: Thanks for calling tech support. How may I help you?
Caller: Hi, my Blackberry screen is white with a pink line down the middle of it.
Agent: Did anything happen to the phone?
Caller: No.
Agent: Does the screen look discolored when it is off?
Caller: Yes.
Agent: The screen is most likely cracked. We will need to send it in for repair.
Caller: Well, it does change colors when I push down on the screen.
Agent (thinking): I guess it doesn't matter at this point.

WHEN DOESN'T IT WORK?

Agent: Thanks for calling tech support. How may I help you?
Caller: Yes, my daughter's TV doesn't have any volume.
Agent: Okay, are you trying to use the remote or the buttons on the TV?
Caller: Well, I tried using the remote.
Agent: Okay, try using the buttons on the TV, and see if the volume works.
Caller: Okay, but I don't understand! It worked perfectly when it was off!

DVD FAIL

Agent: Thanks for calling tech support. How may I help you?
Caller: Hi, I need to order a CD drive because my computer only has a DVD drive.
Agent: Have you tried putting the CD in the DVD drive?
Caller: No.
Agent: DVD drives will play CDs but not the other way around.

Caller puts the CD in the DVD drive, and the music plays.

PROOF THAT 12/21/12 IS NOT THE END!

This is a picture of someone's computer showing that Adobe was last used on May of 2071.

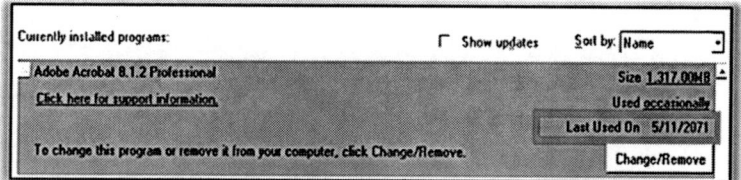

NO, IT'S THE WOMEN'S URINAL

Maintenance: Facilities, how can I help you?

Agent: Hey, man, we have one of the urinals overflowing on our floor.

Maintenance: Okay, I'll get someone down there. Is it in the men's or the women's restroom?

Agent: ...The men's.

YUMMY

Agent: Thanks for calling tech support. How may I help you?
Caller: Yes, I'm a service technician, and I just completed a service call.
Agent: Okay, how can I help you?
Caller: I wanted you to know that I don't care how many more times they dispatch us out to this house we will not service the unit! Every time I come out here, I have to clean off my shoes before I get back in the truck. This house is filthy. The unit is not serviceable because it is an environmental hazard. There are roaches in that dryer! There are literally hundreds of roaches pouring out of the dryer! That's why it doesn't work! So if they call in again, you can explain that it is not covered because we will not go back out to that house!
Agent: I'll notate the account.

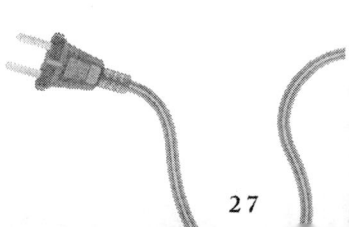

SHE'S A REAL KNOCKOUT!

Agent: Thanks for calling tech support. How may I help you?

Caller: Hi, my ex-girlfriend got mad at me and knocked me out with my laptop. When I woke up, there was a crack on the screen. So I need you to get me a new laptop.

Agent: Sir, I apologize, but your warranty does not cover physical damage.

Caller: What! What kind of show are you running! I want to speak with your supervisor, now!

Agent: Bear with me one moment while I get a supervisor.

Supervisor: Hello, sir, how may I help you?

Caller: Yes, my gal knocked the laptop upside my head, and you're going to send me a new one!

Supervisor: Sir, your warranty covers manufacturer defects. It does not cover physical damage. I'm sorry but we cannot send you a new laptop.

Caller: The warranty is supposed to cover everything, lightning strikes, volcano-like eruptions, earthquakes, and hurricanes around my house!

Supervisor: Sir, the warranty does not cover acts of God or ex-girlfriends.

IT'S THE SIMPLE THINGS

Agent: Thanks for calling tech support. How may I help you?
Caller: Hello there. I set a password, and now, I can't login to the computer.
Agent: Okay, if you can't remember the password, we'll need to reinstall Windows to clear it.
Caller: No. No. I know the password. But when I type it in, nothing happens.
Agent: Sir, you know the password?
Caller: Yes.
Agent: Sir, type in the password.
Caller: Okay.
Agent: Now press Enter.
Caller: Oh.

YES, WE GET PRANK CALLS

New-Hire Agent: Thanks for calling tech support. How may I help you?
Caller (faking an oriental accent): Hi, I need to register my a-port-a-potty!
New-Hire Agent: Okay.
Caller: You have very a pretty voice!
New-Hire Agent: Excuse me?
Caller: You have a voice like an angel!

New-Hire Agent puts caller on Hold and transfers the caller to her supervisor.

Caller: Hello?
Supervisor: Hello.
Caller: Hey, what just happened? I call to register port-a-potty, and she disappeared! Put her back!
Supervisor: She transferred the call to me because you were hitting on her.
Caller: What! I been happily married forty year! Why would I hit on her! I just pay compliment!
Supervisor: And our client doesn't sell port-a-potties.
Click.

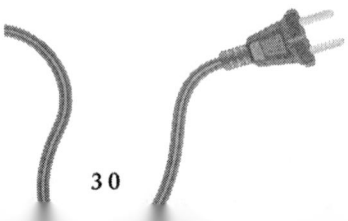

FLIP FLOP

Agent: Thanks for calling tech support. How may I help you?
Caller: Hi. I accidently stepped on my headphones and cracked them.
Agent: I apologize, sir, but your warranty does not cover accidental damage.
Caller: Okay, I didn't step on them. They just stopped working.
Agent: Sir, you've already told me you stepped on them.
Caller: Well, I didn't.
Agent: Sir, even if I did send them in for replacement, you would get charged because they would be damaged.
Click.

Caller calls back and gets the same agent.

Agent: Thanks for calling tech support. How may I help you?
Caller: Hi. My headphones just stopped working.
Agent: Sir, this is the same agent. I just talked with you about this.
Caller: Oh.
Click.

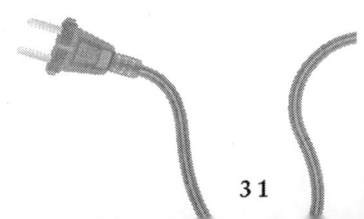

LYING DOESN'T PAY

Another Agent: Thanks for calling tech support. How may I help you?
Caller: Hi. My headphones stopped working.
Agent: What are they doing?
Caller: The left ear doesn't work.
Agent: Is there any damage?
Caller: No, they just stopped working.
Agent: Okay, we'll send you a check so you can replace the headset. You should receive it within ten business days. There will be return labels so you can send the headset back.
Caller: Okay, thank you.

Caller forgets to hang-up and starts talking to his friend in the background.

Caller: Ha! Yes! It worked! As soon as I get that check, I'm cashing it so that I get the money before they realize I stepped on the dumb thing!
Caller's friend: Ha ha, nice, then they won't have time to cancel it!

The agent continues to listen to the conversation and notates it in detail on the account that the caller admitted to the headset being damaged and cancelled the check.

FREEZING HOT

Agent: Thanks for calling tech support. How may I help you?
Caller: Hi, my laptop keeps freezing up! It's getting worse and worse, and the keyboard is also very hot.
Agent: Was your power adapter replaced recently?
Caller: Yes.
Agent: Try unplugging the power cord from the computer.
Caller: Well, now it's acting normal.
Agent: Plug the AC adapter back in, and see if it starts freezing again.
Caller: Yeah, it's freezing again. Why would the AC adapter do that?
Agent: On the bottom of your AC adapter, does it say 90 watt or 60 watt?
Caller: Ninety.
Agent: Your computer was made for a 60-watt adapter. I would return that adapter and get a 60 watt. Unfortunately, this happens often. The wattage does matter. Make sure you are buying the same kind that came with your computer originally when you replace a power adapter.

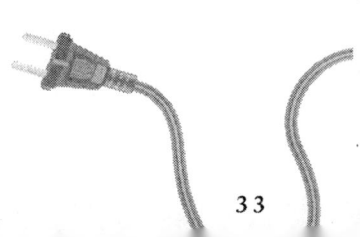

CHOCOLATE AND GRIEF COUNSELING

Agent: Thanks for calling tech support. How may I help you?

Caller: I require chocolate and grief counseling. My computer is very slow and will not reinstall my virus scan software. It gives me random fits as well. I have asked it many times. Was it worth it? Because despite your violent behavior, the only thing you've managed to break so far is my heart. Maybe you could settle for that!

Agent: Is it freezing a lot?

Caller: Yes, but when I put the blankets on, her temperature only gets worse.

Agent: Has it given you any error messages?

Caller: She has scribed one letter. It reads:

> Dear, sir,
>
> I am gone. My disk is nay to be found, lost at sea forever. You may try my CD drive, but that is only the hand waving. Cursed are you to have lost me.

Agent: ...Sounds like a bad hard drive. I'll set it up for repair.

KNOWING YOUR INS AND OUTS

Agent: Thanks for calling tech support. How may I help you?
Caller: When I plug my mp3 player into the stereo where it says "Line In," it won't charge.

Note: Customer is going from an audio output to an audio input on another device.

Agent: Ma'am, the line-in input is not used for charging things. It's an audio input.
Caller: No. It plays fine, but it won't stay charged.
Agent: You need to plug the power cord into the bottom of the mp3 player so that both the audio cord and the power cord are plugged in at the same time.
Caller: Oh. You can do that?
Agent: Yes.

UNDER COMMUNICATOR-N-ING

Agent: Thanks for calling tech support. How may I help you?
Caller: Hi. My washer's broke.
Agent: Who is the manufacturer of the washer?
Caller: Uh, the appliance store.
Agent: No, I mean who made it, not where it was purchased.
Caller: The appliance store!
Agent: What was the price?
Caller: The appliance store, is that what you need?

HUE NEED GLASSES

Agent: Thanks for calling tech support. How may I help you?
Caller: When I print to color, the end result looks odd. The colors are just off, and they seem to be dominated by one color.
Agent: Could you scan us a copy of what is being printed so we can see it?
Caller: Sure, I'll scan it and send it to you.
Agent: Okay.

Caller scans the printout and attaches it to an e-mail, then sends us the e-mail.

Agent: Sir, open up that picture that you sent us.
Caller: Okay.
Agent: Does it look exactly like the one you had printed?
Caller: Yes.
Agent: Sir, it's in black and white.

ANYONE HAVE A CVD?

Agent: Thanks for calling tech support. How may I help you?
Caller: My CD drive does not play my DVDs.
Agent: That's correct.

Note: DVDs can play CDs, but it does not work the other way around.

THE POWER OF THE POWER BUTTON

Agent: Thanks for calling tech support. How may I help you?
Caller: I am not able to see my monitor!
Agent: Push the Power button on the bottom of the monitor.

Caller pushes the power button and the monitor turns on.

Caller: Oh, wow, you guys are good!

COMMA, ON!

Online Web Ticket

Customer: When,I,type,and,hit,the,space,bar,there's,a, comma,after,every,word,this,is,happening,in, every, program,

Agent E-mail: Check your keyboard and see if there is anything stuck in the keys.

Customer: I found something stuck under the space bar!

THE INDEFINITE LOOP

Agent: Thanks for calling tech support. How may I help you?
Caller: I cannot remote into my computer.
Agent: Please give me the computer name that you are trying to remote into, and I'll ping it.
Caller: My computer name is ABC-1234.
Agent: I can't get a response from your computer. It is either turned off or not connected to the business network.
Caller: What do you mean it's off? I'm using it right now, but it won't let me remote into it!
Agent: So you are on the computer and you are trying to remote into it?
Caller: Yes.
Agent: Sir, you can't remote into a computer you are currently on. The purpose of remote desktop is to access a different computer.

RECHANGING

Agent: Thanks for calling tech support. How may I help you?
Caller: Instead of resetting my password, can I just change it?
Agent: ...Sure.

Agent walks customer through how to reset or "change" their password.

DISAPPEARING ACT

Agent: Thanks for calling tech support. How may I help you?
Caller: I am unable to see my PowerPoint presentation.
Agent: Let me remote in and take a look.

Agent connects to the customer's computer.

Agent: Your PowerPoint presentation is open.
Caller: I still can't see it.

The agent drags the presentation over from one screen to the other.

Caller: Now I can see it!
Agent: It is on your other screen.
Caller: Oh, I turned that screen off to save energy.

SELECTIVE HEARING

Agent: Thanks for calling tech support. How may I help you?
Caller: Yes, during the middle of my phone calls, the calls tend to drop.
Agent: Okay. What is your phone number?
Caller: 555-234-5678.
Agent: Okay. Have you—
Caller: Hey, I'm getting a call on my cell, and I've got to take this!

Click.

SHUT DOWN A.K.A. OFF

Agent: Thanks for calling tech support. How may I help you?
Caller: I can't remote into a computer.
Agent: I am unable to ping the computer. It is either turned off or is having network issues.
Caller: Well, I shut it down, but I didn't turn it off!
Agent: ...

STEP 3: SEE STEP 1

Agent: Thanks for calling tech support. How may I help you?
Caller: I'm frustrated because I cannot get through the phone activation steps. Step 1 says that there is additional documentation about the device. Why do I want to know about this information? This doesn't make sense! I just want to activate the phone! Step 2 shows even more information, and I can't get to step 3 because step 1 and 2 will take too long to read over this manual about specs and features.
Agent: Skip to step 3.
Caller: Okay, step 3 says to make sure the radio is on. Why do I need a radio? I just want to activate the phone! I don't care if the radio is playing. It doesn't have anything to do with this!
Agent: Does it show 3G on the phone?
Caller: Yes.
Agent: Your radio is on. Let's go to step 4.

Eventually, the phone is activated.

BREAKING GLASS

Agent: Thanks for calling tech support. How may I help you?
Caller: Yes, I need to have someone come and replace the window that I am getting ready to throw this computer out of!
Agent: Sir, it's raining outside. You may want to wait until tomorrow.

THE PRECALL CALL

Agent: Thanks for calling tech support. How may I help you?
Caller: Hi, my computer is not working.
Agent: Okay. May I have your phone number?
Caller: 555-222-3434.
Agent: Thank you. Bear with me for just a moment while I pull up your information.
Caller: Okay, bye.
Agent: Sir, wait!
Click.

MAGNETO MAKES A HOUSE CALL

Local support finishes installing a fourth replacement hard drive at the customer's house.

Customer: You guys have replaced my hard drive three times! Every time you do, it works for a day and then stops working!

Local Support: Okay, ma'am, why don't we stay here for a little bit and see what happens.

Twenty minutes go by, and everything seems normal. Just before local support leaves, the customer starts decorating her computer.

Local Support: Ma'am, are those magnets?
Customer: Yes.
Local Support: Ma'am, you just covered the entire side of your computer in magnets!
Customer: Yes, I did. Why?
Local Support: Ma'am, magnets have a tendency to erase data off hard drives.
Customer: Oh…

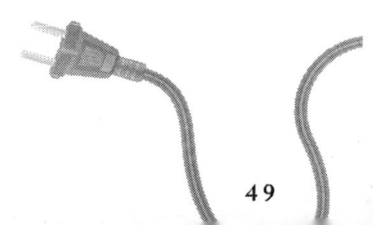

CONCLUSION

Reading these stories may actually give insight to a computer issue you are currently having. Several people have these same issues. It is my hope that by providing these stories, you can realize that tech support agents get these types of calls all the time. If you were embarrassed because something similar happened to you, don't be. You are not alone. Tech support exists because we understand that people need help.

On the flip side, just because tech support agents are available, that does not mean they are allowed or even know how to help with every issue. We are imperfect beings, like everyone else. Even tech support agents need tech support sometimes. Many times, agents have a predefined "scope of support" that they are not allowed to go outside of. I hope you understand after reading this that the reason that scope is defined is because if it wasn't, frankly, everyone would be calling. Wait times would be hours upon hours.

These are just people trying to make a living. They are not scapegoats designated to take verbal beatings all day. They are here to help. If they can't help with something because it is outside the company's defined scope, that doesn't mean they don't want to. It means they may be fired if they do. Would you sacrifice your monthly income to help someone do something that you are not supposed to help them with?

Next time you find yourself yelling at someone on the phone, ask yourself if you are being selfish. If you are trying to get someone to help you at the expense of their income, you are.

TROUBLESHOOTING GUIDE

The following pages will take you through the same troubleshooting steps that tech support would guide you through.

These troubleshooting steps are not guaranteed to fix all issues. They are designed to fix the more common errors end users receive.

TROUBLESHOOTING POWER ISSUES

ERROR: NOTHING HAPPENS AT ALL WHEN YOU PUSH THE POWER BUTTON

Desktops:

1. Disconnect the power cord from the wall and the computer.
2. With the power cord still completely disconnected, press and hold down the Power button for ten seconds. (Yes, this sounds strange, but it will release any static buildup in the computer.)
3. Plug the power cord firmly into the computer.
4. Connect the other end of the power to a different power outlet. Sockets in a multiple outlet extension cord can go bad. I recommend plugging directly into the wall for troubleshooting purposes.
5. If nothing is lighting up, disconnect the power cord from the wall outlet. Plug in a light or something else into that wall outlet to verify that it is working. If that unit works, plug the computer back into that wall outlet.
6. If the lights on the computer are turned on but nothing displays on the screen, skip to step 7. If absolutely nothing is turning on, look at the back of the computer. There should be a light near where the power cord plugs into the computer. This light indicates that the power

supply is getting power. If there is a light and it is on, the motherboard needs to replaced or repaired. If there is a light and it is off or there is no light at all and no fan noise, replace the power supply. (If you are not a tech, this is the point where you take it to the repair shop.)

7. If the computer has lights on, make sure the monitor is on. (Move to the section called "Monitor Says 'No Signal' or Does Not Display Anything.")

Laptops:

1. Disconnect the power cord from the wall and the computer. (Also disconnect it from the adapter if the adapter and the cord are separate parts.)
2. Pull out the battery.
3. With the power cord and battery still completely disconnected, press and hold down the power button for ten seconds. (Yes, this sounds strange, but it will release any static buildup in the computer.)
4. Inspect the power input on the computer for a loose or missing power pin. If the power pin is missing or feels loose when you connect the power cord, the computer needs to be repaired. (Skip the rest of the trouble shooting and take the computer to the repair shop.) If it is not loose or missing, continue to step 5.
5. Plug the adapter firmly into the computer. (If the adapter and the power cord are separate, plug the power cord firmly into the adapter.)

6. Connect the other end of the power to a different power outlet. (Sockets in a multiple outlet extension cord can go bad. I recommend plugging directly into the wall for troubleshooting purposes.)
7. If nothing is turning on, disconnect the power cord from the wall outlet. Plug in a light or something else into that wall outlet to verify that it is working. If that unit works, plug the computer back into that wall outlet.
8. If no lights turn on, on the computer, check the adapter. If the adapter normally has a light on it and it is not lit or the adapter feels cold after being plugged in for five minutes, replace the adapter. (Keep the receipt. If it still doesn't turn on with a new adapter, return the adapter, and take the computer to a repair shop).
9. If the adapter shows signs that it has power (it has a light on it or it feels warm after five minutes) and still no lights on the computer, send the computer in for repair.
10. If the lights on the computer turn on but the screen does not light up, try pressing the Caps Lock button. If the Caps Lock light comes on but nothing displays on the screen, try pressing the function key, FN, and F4, F5 or F6 together. If it still does not display, most likely, there is a loose internal video connection, or the screen needs to be replaced. Take the laptop to a repair tech. (If the tech says the screen needs to be replaced, most of the time, it is cheaper to buy a new computer. Get a quote before you give them the go-ahead to repair it.) If the Caps

Lock light does not come, the motherboard needs to be replaced. Take the computer to a repair tech.

ERROR: MONITOR SAYS "NO SIGNAL" OR DOES NOT DISPLAY ANYTHING

Desktops:

1. Make sure the computer is on. If there are no lights on the computer, go back to the section called "Nothing Happens at All when You Push the Power Button." If there are lights on the computer, continue to step 2.
2. Try pressing the Caps Lock button. If the Caps Lock light comes on, continue to step 3. If it does not turn on, take the computer to a repair shop.
3. Disconnect the power cord from the monitor.
4. With the power cord disconnected from the monitor screen, press and hold down the Power button on the monitor screen for ten seconds. (Yes, this sounds strange, but it will release any static buildup in the monitor.)
5. Reconnect the power cord to the monitor screen firmly.
6. Press the Power button. If the light on the screen stays green or blue but it does not display, try connecting a different monitor screen (if possible). If this is not possible, take the screen to a repair shop and have them connect it to a computer and turn it on before you leave. If it displays, then it is the computer that needs to be repaired, not the screen. If it does not display, the screen

is bad. If the light turns amber or you get a message that says "No Signal," skip to step 7.
7. Disconnect and reconnect the video cable from the computer and the screen. (This is usually the cord with two screws plugged into the back of the monitor screen.)
8. If the same thing occurs, try a different video cable.
9. If the same thing occurs, try connecting a different monitor screen (if possible). If this is not possible, take the screen to a repair shop and have them connect it to a computer and turn it on before you leave. If it displays, then it is the computer that needs to be repaired, not the screen. If it does not display, the screen is bad.

Laptops:

1. Disconnect the power cord from the wall and the computer. (Also disconnect it from the adapter, if the adapter and the cord are separate parts)
2. Pull out the battery.
3. With the power cord and battery still completely disconnected, press and hold down the Power button for ten seconds. (Yes, this sounds strange, but it will release any static buildup in the computer.)
4. Plug the adapter firmly into the computer. (If the adapter and the power cord are separate, plug the power cord firmly into the adapter.)
5. Connect the other end of the power to the power outlet.

6. If the lights on the computer turn on but the screen does not light up, try pressing the Caps Lock button. If the Caps Lock light comes on but nothing displays on the screen, most likely, there is a loose connection or the screen needs to be replaced. Take the laptop to a repair tech. If the tech says the screen needs to be replaced, most of the time, it is cheaper to buy a new computer. Get a quote before you give them the go-ahead to repair it. If the Caps Lock light does not come, the motherboard needs to be replaced. Take the computer to a repair tech.

ERROR: BATTERY LIGHT FLASHES, BUT NOTHING ELSE HAPPENS

Laptops:

1. Plug the adapter in.
2. If the laptop does not turn on, go back to the section called "Nothing Happens at All when You Push the Power Button."

ERROR: COMPUTER GETS HOT AND SHUTS OFF

Desktops:

1. Clean all of the vents or fans with an air compressed duster.
2. If it continues to overheat and you are not a technician, take the computer to a repair shop.

Reboot

Laptops:

If you just bought a new AC adapter and this starts happening, return it immediately. The two most common types of adapters are a 65-watt and a 90-watt. You probably bought the wrong kind. Make sure you have a sales rep look up the specs on your adapter from the manufacturer's website before buying from the rep.

1. What type of surface is the computer on? Blankets, pillows, and carpet could cause the computer to collect heat. Don't place the computer on these surfaces. Place it on a hard, flat surface that does not collect heat.
2. Clean all the vents or fans with an air compressed duster.
3. If it continues to overheat and you are not a technician, take the computer to a repair shop.

ERROR: COMPUTER TURNS ON BUT NOTHING SHOWS ON THE SCREEN

Desktops:

1. If the lights on the computer turn on but the screen does not light up, try pressing the Caps Lock button. If the Caps Lock light comes on, go back to the section called "Monitor Says, 'No Signal' or Does Not Display Anything." If the Caps Lock light does not come on, the motherboard needs to be repaired or replaced. Send the computer in for repair.

Laptops:

1. Try pressing the function key, FN, and F4, F5 or F6 together. If this does not work, press the same key again and go back to the section called "Monitor Says, 'No Signal' or Does Not Display Anything."

TROUBLESHOOTING NETWORK ISSUES

ERROR: INTERNET EXPLORER CANNOT DISPLAY THE WEBPAGE

1. Click on Tools. (It's usually in the top left or right of the Internet Explorer window.)
2. Click Internet Options or Internet Properties.
3. Click Delete. The only three things that need to be checked are Temporary Internet Files, Cookies, and History.
4. Make sure only those three are checked. (Uncheck Preserve Favorites Website Data. This will not delete your actual favorites.)
5. Click Delete.
6. Close all Internet Explorer windows, and reopen Internet Explorer.
7. If the problem continues, try going to a different website. If the issue still continues, skip to the section called "I Cannot See Any Available Networks or It Says I'm Disconnected."

ERROR: ACCESS LOCAL ONLY

1. You most likely typed in the wrong passphrase, password, or passkey for the network you connected to. Disconnect

from the network and then try to reconnect to it so that it asks you for the security key again.
2. Skip to "I Cannot See Any Available Networks or It Says I'm Disconnected."

ERROR: I CANNOT SEE ANY AVAILABLE NETWORKS OR IT SAYS I'M DISCONNECTED

Desktops:

1. Unplug the power cord from the back of your router (if you have one) and/or your modem. (If you have a modem with a battery backup, you will need to pull the batteries out too.) Wait for a few seconds, and then plug the power cords back in. Once the lights are all back up again, try to reopen Internet Explorer.
2. Press and hold ⊞ and R. The Run window should appear.
3. Type in "devmgmt.msc" and click OK.
4. Double click on Network Adapters, and then right-click all the devices listed under that section, and choose Uninstall.
5. Once the listing Network Adapters has disappeared, restart your computer.
6. It will automatically reinstall. If the issue continues, call your Internet service provider before taking the computer in for repair.

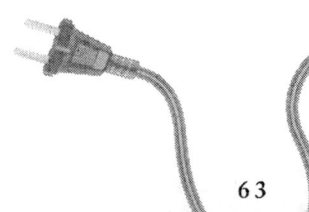

Laptops:

1. On all laptops, there is a wireless switch. The switch generally is either on the side or front of the computer and looks like a sliding button or is on top, above the keyboard, and looks like a button satellite symbol. Make sure that switch is on.
2. Unplug the power cord from the back of your router (if you have one) and/or your modem. (If you have a modem with a battery backup, you will need to pull the batteries out too.) Wait for a few seconds, then plug the power cords back in. Once the lights are all back up again, try to reopen Internet Explorer.
3. Press and hold ⊞ and R. The Run window should appear.
4. Type in "devmgmt.msc" and click OK.
5. Double click on Network Adapters, and then right-click all the devices listed under that section, and choose Uninstall.
6. Once the listing Network Adapters has disappeared, restart your computer.
7. It will automatically reinstall. If the issue continues, call your Internet service provider, before taking the computer in for repair.

TROUBLESHOOTING CD/DVD ISSUES

ERROR: CD/DVD DRIVE WILL EITHER PLAY CDS AND NOT DVDS, VICE-VERSA OR NOT BURN CDS/DVDS BUT WILL PLAY

Vista Only:

1. Go to http://support.microsoft.com/kb/929461.
2. Skip to the below steps for XP and Windows7.

XP and Windows 7:

1. Press and hold ⊞ and R. The Run window should appear.
2. Type in "devmgmt.msc" and click OK.
3. Double click on DVD/CD-ROM drives, and then right-click the CD and DVD devices, and choose Uninstall.
4. Once the listing has disappeared, restart your computer.
5. It will automatically reinstall. If the issue continues, take it in for repair.

ERROR: CD/DVD DRIVE HAS DISAPPEARED FROM THE LIST UNDER MY COMPUTER

Vista Only:

1. Go to http://support.microsoft.com/kb/929461.
2. Skip to the below steps for XP and Windows7.

XP and Windows 7:

1. Press and hold ⊞ and R. The Run window should appear.
2. Type in "devmgmt.msc" and click OK.
3. Double click on DVD/CD-ROM drives, and then right-click the CD and DVD devices, and choose Uninstall.
4. Once the listing has disappeared, restart your computer.
5. It will automatically reinstall. If the issue continues, take it in for repair.

ERROR: CD/DVD WILL NOT PLAY AT ALL

Vista Only:

1. Go to http://support.microsoft.com/kb/929461.
2. Skip to the below steps for XP and Windows7.

XP and Windows 7:

1. Press and hold ⊞ and R. The Run window should appear.
2. Type in "devmgmt.msc" and click OK.

3. Double click on DVD/CD-ROM drives, and then right-click the CD and DVD devices, and choose Uninstall.
4. Once the listing has disappeared, restart your computer.
5. It will automatically reinstall. If the issue continues, take it in for repair.

ERROR: CD/DVD DRIVE WILL NOT OPEN/EJECT

Restart the computer. If it still will not open, the CD/DVD drive needs to be replaced or reseated by a technician.

TROUBLESHOOTING PRINTER ISSUES

ERROR: ANY ERROR WHILE ATTEMPTING TO PRINT

1. Ensure the proper printer is selected. Press and hold ⊞ and R. The Run window should appear.
2. Type in "Control Printers" and press Enter.
3. Verify the printer you want to print to is set as the default. If it is not, right click and choose Set as Default Printer.
4. If the error continues, press and hold ⊞ and R. The Run window should appear.
5. Type in "Control admintools" and press Enter.
6. Click on Services.
7. Look for Printer Spooler and verify that it says "Started" next to it. If it does not, right click on Printer Spooler and choose Start. Close this window afterward.
8. Restart the computer and the printer. (For wireless printers, you may want to also unplug the power cord to the router and plug it back in.)
9. Remove and Reinstall the printer using the instructions from the manufacturer's website.

TROUBLESHOOTING MICROSOFT OFFICE

ERROR: ANY ERROR

1. Save whatever you are working on and close all Microsoft Office programs.
2. Press and hold ⊞ and R. The Run window should appear.
3. Type in "appwiz.cpl" and press Enter.
4. Find the version of the Microsoft Office Suite you have installed, and select it. Then choose Change.
5. Select the prompts to Repair office.
6. Once the repair is complete, try restarting the computer.

TROUBLESHOOTING VIRUS/MALWARE

1. Run a full virus scan if you have virus scan software available. Do not purchase any virus scan software if there is a pop-up saying you need to in order to fix the problem. That is all part of the scam. Only run the virus scan software that you had prior to receiving the virus.
2. Press and hold ⊞ and R. The Run window should appear.
3. Type in "rstrui.exe" and press Enter.
4. Click Next and select a date that is one day or more prior to receiving the virus.
5. Follow the rest of the prompts to restore windows to an earlier date. This will restart the computer, so make sure everything is saved and all programs are closed.
6. Once the repair is complete, if the virus is still there, take the computer to a repair tech to have everything backed up and the computer wiped.

Note: The steps 1–6 will not delete any data, but it may uninstall a program, if the installation of the program was after the date selected.

DELETING EVERYTHING AND STARTING OVER RUNNING RECOVERY

Most computers built after 2007 have a recovery partition. This will delete everything.

1. Turn the computer off and back on. The very first screen that appears is the splash screen. It does not last long. Press the Pause key to stop it from changing to the next screen. This should tell you what keys to press to run recovery.
2. Press the keys listed together.
3. Follow the prompts.

If your computer's splash screen does not list any combination to press to run recovery, review the documentation on your manufacturer's website. Additionally, if you have run operating system discs previously to either upgrade or reinstall the operating system, that recovery partition is likely gone and recovery discs will be required in order to run recovery.

CPSIA information can be obtained at www.ICGtesting.com
Printed in the USA
LVOW10s0931030214

372069LV00001B/4/P